The Bible and Your Life

The Bible and Your Life

Frank Pollard

BROADMAN PRESS
Nashville, Tennessee

4251-66
ISBN: 0-8054-5166-8

Printed in the United States of America

Dedicated

in loving appreciation
to
Dr. and Mrs. P. D. O'Brien

Preface

Michelangelo saw a discarded lump of marble in a builder's yard. It was stained, mishapen and unattractive. He said to the builder: "Take it to my studio, there is an angel in that marble and I can set it free!"

Jesus Christ, the leader of The Human Liberation Movement, sees our stained and mishapen lives. Looking through the ugly, amateurish chips occasioned by our puny efforts to shape a life He says: "Give that life to me. There is a successful person in there and I can set him free!"

These chapters have come from years of personal struggle with life's real meaning and from soul-searching dialogue with fellow strugglers. I have seen men energetically set out for success in the 1,001 varieties of ways this world offers it. The most pitiful pictures in the showcase of misused life are those who have attained their goals of things, fame, pleasure or whatever and found no satisfaction in either the journey or the arrival.

All the while The Human Liberation Leader offers "abundant life," consisting of joy, peace, purpose, power and riches that cannot be stolen, lost or depreciated.

He not only can give you a successful life — He can help you know that you have it!

Contents

The Bible and Your Life

CHAPTER ONE

The Bible and Your Success

From border to border this country is filled with folk, out of breath, whose sides are aching from hard running, trying to get ahead without thinking about what is ahead. They race in determined fashion down a road marked "This Way to Success" with only a vague idea of where they will be if they get there.

What in God's world is success? That is our question. In this planet of wholesale business, everyone wants to be successful, but what is it? From border to border this country is filled with folk, out of breath, whose sides are aching from hard running, trying to get ahead without thinking about what is ahead. They race in determined fashion down a road marked, "this way to success" with only a vague idea of where they will be if they get there.

Some say, "When I get there I will be rich," meaning they will have a lot of money. Often the acquiring of money and its derivatives is the consuming passion of the best days of life. In younger days I bought a book entitled *Think and Grow Rich.* It is not a bad book. It contains some very good advice even for those who do not think in dollar signs. The foreword said a great secret was written between the lines and as a reader when I discovered the secret I was well on my way to being rich. The secret was easily found — it was greed — grubby, grasping greed. The thesis of the book *Think and Grow Rich* is that all you're supposed to think about is growing rich. Have you noticed how much literature is sold promising to make people rich? The ones that kind of business make rich are the people who sell the literature. From a radio station across the Rio Grande came this commercial: "Send me 25 cents and I will tell you how I became a millionaire." The answer: "I became a millionaire by asking people to send me twenty-five cents."

Some say position is success. To be the leader, the top dog. Of course the top banana gets more money than the rest of the bunch, so it comes back to that.

Others might shun being the chief or bringing in the cash, and define success as pleasure seeking, freedom to exploit every pleasure.

The truth is, a one-world man chasing success would combine all of these, plus a few more. Long before Hugh Hefner dressed the ancient pagan religion of Hedonism in twentieth-century garb and got gullible guys hopping down the bunny trail, there was a playboy who would make Hugh Hefner look like Bishop Sheen by contrast. This fellow was the absolute monarch of a powerful nation. His reputation for riches, revelry and wisdom was known around the world. He wrote an autobiography. It is called Ecclesiastes. It is in the Old Testament. In this moving testimony of the scandal of a wasted life, King Solomon said, "I have tried it all, luxury, learning, liquor, lust, and my life is empty. All too late," said sad Solomon, "I discovered some things." As do most all well-known people who make mistakes, he passed on a word to others setting out for success. "Remember now thy Creator in the day of thy youth."

Meanwhile, out in the woods, wandering from flower to flower is the anti-success creature. He has no idea what success is either, but he is sure he does not want to pay the price to get it. His vocabulary is different. What he calls "playing it cool" the Bible calls idleness and we call laziness. To him his inactivity and star-gazing, non-productiveness borders on spiritual perfection, but the Bible says it is sin. At any rate this fellow thinks he is succeeding by trying not to.

The truth is, all of us want to succeed in life. The Apostles were not exceptions. James and John, Sons of Thunder, who had caused many rumblings on the seashore were now the cause of a social thunderstorm among the Apostles. They had launched a campaign for the number one and two positions in the kind of kingdom they supposed our Lord would set up.

Here is a common picture. Two young men striving to get ahead in their chosen field. And Jesus did not react with anger or displeasure. He lovingly told them that because they did not understand his mission or his kingdom, they did not know what they were asking.

Does it bother you to face the fact that by most of our standards Jesus was a failure? He was highly motivated, hard-working. Remember how his mother worried about His working too hard? There is no doubting his ability to lead and inspire men. He could have been one of the wealthiest of all people. When His fame spread, He was not too impressed by popularity. When He lovingly healed people He asked them not to say who did it. He apparently desired no title, honor or position. Yet there was an aura of success about Him. He knew and promised successful life. He called it the abundant life.

I. This lesson He taught about successful living.

Security is in knowing God. We have to feel secure don't we? At least we want to very badly. There is sort of a dependent nature built into us. Adam and Eve felt a great security in their fellowship with God in Eden, but when their sin separated them from God the security was gone.

When a man's sins separate him from God, a kind of terror begins to grip him. He is alone with other people with no visible means of support. He has no one to pray to but himself. Having lost the security of belonging to God, he grasps for security in things. Like a child in the dark he needs a security blanket, something to hold to. Like Linus in the Peanuts cartoon, many a man clutches his security blanket. He drives a big, nice car; that reminds of his "security." He keeps his check book in hand; the balance is his security blanket. He knows at all times where he can get his hands on title deeds because things have become his security blanket.

Advertising takes advantage of man's security blanket complex. Arnold Toynbee said; "Advertising is the art of taking advantage of human silliness." We buy things from each other we do not want, at prices we cannot pay, on terms we cannot meet because of advertising we do not believe.

Status seeking, getting more things to prove your worth, to enhance your security, produces a state of restless insecurity. Sin always lies. In this case it promises security and produces insecurity. This traps people in a sort of economic purgatory between the supposed hell of the hopelessly poor and the imagined heaven of the entrenched rich.

Jesus came to free people from this insecurity and give real security. Have you noticed how Jesus dealt with wealthy people? It is important to note He did not denounce wealth as wrong. It is morally neutral. It can be used to do good or evil. Two questions are important about a man and his wealth. How did he get it, and what is he going to do with it now that he has it? Jesus did not ask every wealthy man He met to sell his goods and give to the poor. When He did ask a man to do that, it was apparent this man thought he owned his things, but really his things owned him and Jesus was trying to free him from a cruel master.

A close study of Jesus' teachings about wealth causes us to think maybe the church is presenting the wrong primary reasons for giving. Or, as my English teacher would say, placing the emphasis on the wrong syllable. We have stressed the importance of separating you from your money because of what can be done with the money—and this is very important. It costs the church just as many cents per kilowatt hour as the grocery store. But the real concern should be you and the constant danger that your things may become your god. As you give part of your toil, your time and yourself, which is all money is, you are avoiding that danger.

Jesus came to give a security that is real. To show us that success is not a matter of struggling to get ahead. The successful man is the one who is free from the killing anxiety of trying to get ahead. Man's life is made secure not by things but by triumph over things. The only real prosperity is in belonging to God.

II. Also involved in Jesus' teachings concerning successful living is this fact: People Are More Important Than Position.

When we talk of people we usually mean other people, but right now I am talking about you and me—"us" people.

There was a church business meeting where someone stood up and made a motion that the preacher quit lying in the pulpit. And the motion failed. I don't know what that means either. I said that to say this:

Just lately, underscoring my great thanks to God for being pastor of this church, I said, in all sincerity that I was not so impressed with me, but supremely impressed with my position. Now I discover this does not reflect what God's Word tells us we are to feel about ourselves. We are to realize that as people we are more important than our position.

Jesus told John and James He was well aware of the world tendency to judge men by their positions of leadership, but these are not His standards.

He is saying that a man is not great because he is president of the United States, but he is great because God made him. You and I do not have to attain any position to become important. We are important because God made us. Our Lord is saying, "You don't have to go out and get security. You have it by faith in God. You don't have to go out and prove your importance, you are important because I made you, I loved you enough to die for you. What other proof would you want of your worth?"

When you are free to see yourself as important then you can be free to see the importance of other people. What a great place to live this would be if all the people did not feel compelled to prove their worth by using others and were free to demonstrate their worth by serving others.

Some piercing lines from T. S. Eliot ask: "When the stranger says, 'What is the meaning of this city? Do you huddle close together because you love each other?' What will you answer? 'We dwell together to make money from each other? or this is a community?' Be prepared for him who knows how to ask questions."

III. Now we are to this third thing. The Secret of Success is being a Servant.

Jesus said: "Fellows, I know you have a yen for greatness. I understand that, I made you that way. I know the world is full of wrong ideas of success or greatness. But inscribe this indelibly on your hearts. He who would be greatest among you must become servant of all."

The Gospel of John tells us that when Jesus came into that upper room He knew He had all authority in heaven and on earth in His hands. Now, here they were, at this very crucial meeting. The Apostles were not prepared for a cross, they were expecting a throne. Here was Christ, fully aware that all authority on earth and in heaven was in His grasp. What would He do? Knowing the hard hours ahead would He perform some outstanding miracle to impress indelibly upon them who He was? Or would He take a scepter, wield it, wave it and command them to bow down before the Lord of Lords to whom God has given all authority in heaven and on earth?

Not a scepter He takes but a towel. Ridding himself of his outer garment He wrapped that towel around His waist, only a slave did that, got a basin of water and one by one He washed the grimy feet of those men.

When He finished He said, "You have called me Lord and Master and that is right. If I, your Lord and Master, have washed your feet then you ought to wash each other's feet."

In this totally unexpected and fantastic way, He was illustrating a truth He constantly lived. God's idea of a man is a servant. In the economy of our Lord there is no future for the boss or for the tyrant, only for those who are willing to serve in the best interest of others.

It is a wise and successful man indeed who does not feel threatened, does not have to prove himself and through the grace of God is free to live a life of service.

In concluding let's underscore a fact Jesus taught about success. There may be nothing wrong with your having money, but if that is all you have you are poor indeed.

Remember the rich farmer of Luke 12? Our Lord did not criticize his making a good crop, or building a bigger barn. He called him foolish because the man could only offer himself eat and drink and this world's pleasure. So when his time ran out he was foolishly poor.

Any successful man has an eye to the future. The person who has the Lord Jesus Christ has the best of both worlds. The man who has only the things of this world for his god has a second-rate life and for his future, hell.

Paul said what only a Christian can say: "To me to live is Christ and to die is gain." What is it to you to live and what will that produce when you die?

Do you say, To me to live is money and to die is . . .

or To me to live is pleasure and to die is . . .

You can say, "To me to live is Christ and to die is gain."

CHAPTER TWO

The Bible and Your World

We know we are made in God's image, thus we are spiritual. Also we are made of earth, to live on earth, so we are material. How do we reconcile dust and deity? How can we cope with being both material and spiritual? Each Christian struggles with the question: "How in Heaven's name do I treat earth's' things?"

Every Christian is a citizen of two worlds. And those worlds are so different! In our best moments we know that both worlds, then and now, are to be committed to Him—that Christian consistency commands commitment of every part of our lives.

So there comes a time when a follower of Christ must ask: "How do I feel about things? If I love Christ, how do I feel about my car? If He is my Master, how do I treat my money? I know I'm not supposed to love things and worship them. Does this mean I have to hate things and spurn them?"

This is not a question with an easy, pat, glib answer. We know we are made in God's image, thus we are spiritual. Also we are aware of being made of earth, to live on earth, so we are material. How do you reconcile dust and deity? How can we cope with being both material and spiritual? Each Christian struggles with the question: "How in Heaven's name do I treat earth's things?"

To find God's answer we go all the way back to the inauguration of the universe. The first words of our Bibles tell us of the purpose and plan of the Creator who brought earth and its things into being, made man out of dust—breathed him into him deity, thus placing him in the middle, linked both to God and to things. He is man in the middle, made in the image of God, made manager of God's things and it becomes apparent that God intends man to thoroughly enjoy the whole process.

I. Man in the middle is made in the image of God.

The beginning paragraphs of scripture picture our benevolent God, happily engaged in the task of creating the universe. It is interesting to note that the Genesis account tells us of the development of life in the exact same order as biological scientists of today would insist. First, vegetation, then marine life, third came bird life, after this, land animals and finally, human life. Only after God had prepared everything necessary for human existence did He say, "Let us make man." Then comes gigantic biblical assertion showing man's great place in creation: "So God created man in His own image."

During the time Moses wrote these lines the function of an image was to represent, say, a king. When a king didn't want his people to forget who was king, he put up images of himself all over the land. These were symbols of his claim to be in sovereign control.

As people made in the image of God, we are His representatives. Man was created to be His vice-regent, charged with the working out of God's will and responsible to God for his actions.

Being made in God's image means He intended us to have a very unusual relatedness to God. Man is not God, but is made like God. Our hearts can feel and love, like His heart. Other animals God created have hearts, but only man's heart-beat here is an echo of His heart-beat there.

It is very evident that God's creative work came to a climax with the creation of man. This is the peak of the pyramid—man is the very pinnacle of creation.

Starting with Genesis 2:4 is the second cycle of the account of the beginning of things. Some have imagined great contradictions between the statements in Genesis 1 and those in Genesis 2. Not so. They are not contradictory, but complementary. They do have different emphasis.

The first account stresses the fact that God in His power and sovereignty created all things. The word create means to originate, to bring into being something distinctly new. It can mean "to make something out of nothing." It refers to something beyond human comprehension or achievement, that which only the God of miracles can do.

The word for God in Genesis 1:1 to 2:3 is the Hebrew word Elohim. The root meaning of Elohim is strength, might and power.

The second account goes on from the creation. It tells how man is related to earth and how man is to have communion with God.

In this second account the Hebrew word for God is Yahweh, which means "God is among His people."

In the first account, man is the peak of creation's pyramid. In the second account he is in the center of creation's circle.

In reaction to the God of creation—he is made in God's image. In relation to the things God created, man is God's representative. He is right in the middle of things and is commanded to "have dominion" over the things God created.

II. So now we can see—Man in the Middle is made manager of God's things.

Adam is placed in the beautiful Garden of Eden, which is God's gracious gift to him. This garden is in the land called Eden, which means "Land of Delight." So here is man, the crown of God's creation—made in His image, placed in the midst of God's creation and told to have dominion. He is to be in charge of things, but he is in charge as one who knows he is taking care of God's things and he is to carry out God's will in the use of those things.

If we could go back to the Garden of Eden, back to those beginning days, knock on the gate and say to Adam, "Who owns this?" He would say, "God owns it." Then if we should say, "Take me to the manager" Adam would reply, "You're talking to him."

This is the right understanding of how God intended we look at things—we are managers of that which belongs to Him. We, like any manager, are responsible to the owner for how we use His things.

The Bible declares in undeniable fashion this great truth: "God has not surrendered title to anything in this world."

Psalm 50: "For every beast of the forest is mine and the cattle on a thousand hills. I know all the birds of the air and all that moves in the field is mine." Psalm 95: "For the Lord is a great God and a great king above all gods. In His hands are the depths of the earth. The heights of the mountains are His also. The sea is His for He made it . . . His hand formed the dry land." Haggai: "The silver is mine and the gold is mine." He just about sums it up in saying to Job: "Whatever is under the whole heaven is mine. (41:11b).

In Jesus' story in Luke 12 of the small barn and the big fool our Lord underscores this fact: "Nothing is really owned that can be lost. No man is wealthy to whom the grave brings bankruptcy." God does not surrender title. It is His.

And Man is made Manager. The Bible word is "steward" or "householder." One who is in charge of looking after the things of another.

May I suggest that this truth takes off a ton of pressure and gives us freedom to enjoy the things God has let us manage.

Here is an illustration: I have a friend who grew up on a West Texas farm. He served in World War II as an infantryman, engaged in combat in Europe. During that time of fighting he had to spend long quiet hours in a fox hole. He thought about his home in West Texas and about farming. One long dark night he pondered the fact that irrigation farming was coming to West Texas and that meant there would be a need for specialized equipment and better seeds. He came back from the war with a vision of a chain of farm and seed stores. But he had no money. For several years he coached and taught school and saved money. His wife taught school. When they had saved $5,000 he and another started a business that made them both millionaires. It stretched across the Plains of Texas and even overseas. I would meet this man and others about six in the morning at a little cafe. He was the most preoccupied, unhappy and worried man I ever knew. The vastness of his business empire was a constant weight upon his shoulders.

Suddenly, one morning he was a different man. He told us he had sold his business to a giant corporation and they had hired him to stay in control. Now he still had the same job, managing the same business, sitting at the same desk working with the same people, and knowing him, he did not let up in dedication to the business. He was a much happier man because now he was a manager, not an owner. Now he was looking after something backed by the brain-power and financial power of a giant corporation. It was no longer just his baby.

A lot of pressure is taken off when you and I realize we are looking after God's things, not ours, and we have the resources of the Creator of this earth behind us. We cannot fail!

There is a great danger in our attitudes and actions concerning money. Many misguided men fail to see things as belonging to God, and sadly enough, things become their god. That's why my friend was so unhappy. He was not able to see his things as God's things so things became his god. You and I have seen poor foolish folk under the terrorizing rules of things and it is no pretty picture. The only release from the tyranny of things is a commitment recognizing that God owns us and He owns what we call ours.

From the outstanding men in the coaching world come testimonies acknowledging God's ownership and their responsibility to Him in managing the things He has let them have.

Frank Broyles of the University of Arkansas asserts: "I am happy to be a tither. My tithe helps my church conduct the Lord's work and it helps me handle more carefully my money and all other gifts with which God has blessed me. I want to be a good steward. Tithing helps me achieve this goal and therefore I recommend it."

Tom Landry of the Dallas Cowboys: "To fully grasp the meaning of stewardship, a Christian must accept the fact that God owns everything. In all of Jesus' references to money one thing is supreme—attitudes. All that Jesus said about money can be summed up in one word, responsibility. A person cannot be a generous steward until he acknowledges the sovereignty of God and accepts his personal responsibility to Him."

III. One other thing is certain from the Genesis account of creation. God made man in His own image. God made man manager of God's things and God intended man to thoroughly enjoy the process.

The Bible tells us God took joy in His work. He would finish a day, look at what He had created and say 'that is good, that is very good'." And God intended man to take joy in His work. He gave man a beautiful garden in which to work. When He saw that man was lonely He gave him a companion. And God was there for man to enjoy. There is no doubt about it, God intended this life to be a happy life for man.

But you remember there was a tree in that garden. That tree was the symbol of God's ownership. And when the Devil lied about that tree and Adam and Eve believed him, they brought sin into their lives and there is never real happiness in a sinful life. Ever since that day people have believed Satan's lie. "You don't really belong to God. You don't need God, you can be your own God." And at one time or another, all of us have believed him and have forfeited the happiness God intended.

But God loved man so much He didn't give up on us. He still wants us to have that joy and that happy fellowship with Him.

That's why Jesus came to die on the cross. That's why He is coming again. God wants us to know the great life He originally planned for us.

When we accept Christ as our personal Lord and Saviour letting Him come in and take over our lives, we have the best kind of life this world has to offer. Yet it is still a struggle and we have to face the presence of sin each day even though we know we are saved from the penalty of sin. But that is not all. One day Jesus is coming again to this earth. And God is going to take over and create a new heaven and a new earth and it will be like He intended in the first place.

The Bible starts with a garden where man and woman and God's things and God are blended into a beautiful fellowship but sin fouled all that up.

Have you noticed how the Bible ends? There is a garden where man and God's things and God are blended into a beautiful fellowship. Only this time sin can't get in.

Don't you miss that.

CHAPTER THREE

The Bible and Your Self-Knowledge

Of course, it's true that almost everybody is a fool to somebody.

A friend called from my home town: "Frank, he said, "We are going to have an All-Fools' Banquet on April first and you are the first one we thought of for a speaker!"

That started me wondering why there is an April Fools' Day. Two encyclopedias agreed it started back in the 1500's when English-speaking people changed calendars. On the old calendar, April 1 was celebrated as New Year's Day. There were some folks around who didn't like their calendar changed any more than some of us like our time to be messed with. So they kept on celebrating New Year's in April instead of January. For this they were called "April Fools' " and finally the day evolved into a time during which you could act foolish and have an excuse for it.

Do you know God's Word warns us about playing the fool in our lives?

Of course it's true that almost everybody is a fool to somebody. To the dyed-in-the-wool Democrat the Republican is a fool. To the hard-core Republican, the Democrat is a fool. The happily-married man tells the bachelor he is foolish to stay single and the unattached fellow thinks it would be idiotic to let a wedding band cut off his circulation. When news leaked out of Fulton's working on a steam powered engine they probably asked him to turn in his high school diploma.

And can't you just hear Edison's wife saying: "Thomas, turn off the light and go to sleep." A lot of people during the Wright Brothers days believed not only flying, but also the Wright Brothers were for the birds. It's true that almost anyone who stands for or tries to do anything is looked upon as foolish by someone.

The Bible tells us how God looks at people. To be called "foolish" or "silly" by someone who is just as foolish and silly is one thing, but to be called "foolish" by God is something altogether different. No less than forty times the Bible aims truth at human frailty and says, "Thou fool!"

That's kind of hard to take isn't it? Somehow it doesn't bother many of us to be called "sinners." We slough it off, mumbling, "Well, nobody's perfect, and after all, the Bible says everyone is a sinner." But to be called "fools," that bites hard at the swollen and touchy nerve of pride.

Yet God's Word constantly levels this accusation—charging all as fools who look too little to God, who look too much to self, and who look down on others.

I. A fool is one who looks all too little to God. He not only ignores God's love and help, but shakes his puny fist in God's face. Such foolish action prompts us to shout: "Silly man, don't box with God, your arms are too short!"

Psalm 53:1 spells it out in unavoidable clarity. "The fool hath said in his heart, 'There is no God'."

A few Christmases ago some American Astronauts looked down while circling the moon, marveled at what they saw and read Scripture from the Book of Genesis. Almost every American thrilled, but at least one bristled. Madilyn Murray O'Hair directed the brain God gave her to the task of seeing He was not ever again praised when so many were listening. The reaction to her reaction was staggering. People everywhere began to publicize their approval of what the Astronauts had done. At this time a committee from the Chamber of Commerce of Tulia, Texas, asked me to write Mrs. O'Hair a letter which would be signed by the people of that city.

Bulldoggedly determined not to be negative, I decided to write her a thank-you note. We thanked her for reminding us that when this nation chooses her best men for a mission, she finds men with deep faith, well trained, scientific men who could look around at a universe and down upon earth and say: "God did that!" We thanked her for reminding us of some facts concerning the philosophy of atheism. Have you noticed? Atheism has never done anything for mankind. How many colleges have been built in the name of atheism? Did you ever see an atheistic memorial hospital? Atheism has never contributed anything but criticism; has never offered anything but offense.

Atheists are miserable little people who go around trying to make others as little and miserable as they are.

A father and his son were committed atheists. For many years they had been firey proponents of the doctrine of no-God. Now the older man lay dying. "Do you think we've made a mistake, son? Do you think there may be a God after all?" The son replied, "Don't give in to those thoughts, Dad, Hold on. Hold on." "That's just it, son, there's not anything to hold on to."

"The fool hath said in his heart, there is no God."

Holy Scripture also labels as "fool" those who play games with God.

The Pharisees, like many a twentieth-century counterpart, were masters at playing church and acting religious at certain times, yet their lives were selfish, sinful and contrary to God's will. In Luke 11:40 Jesus said: "You fools, don't you know God can see right through you?"

Foolish folk who regard God too lightly are prone to mock at sin.

Disregarding His ability to see, even in dark places they foolishly forget that sin always pays its wages. Proverbs 14:9 asserts: "Fools make a mock at sin." They always have. In the Garden of Eden, that subtle con artist said: "Look, Eve, Honey, God was only kidding you. He won't really punish you. Go ahead, try it." In the days before the flood they said, "Noah, you've got water on the brain. We're too far advanced to fall for that 'punishment for sin' bit." But the rain came anyway.

Today, society's garbage heap is littered with the broken lives of those who made a mockery of sin.

II. The fool looks all too little to God and all too much to himself.

Looking upon the folly of a wasted life, one man said: "I lived for myself. Thought for myself. For myself and none beside. Just as if Jesus had never lived, as if He had never died."

The writer of God's wisdom puts it this way in Proverbs 28:26:

"He that trusteth in his own heart is a fool." You see, that is why there is so much mental strain and anguish in this day. All too many are trying to be their own God. No one is big enough, wise enough or strong enough to be his own God, thus the great strain.

The foolish fellow, looking to himself, despises instruction. He's not about to be told anything.

Proverbs 15:5 states: "A fool despises his father's instructions." And that principle can be greatly broadened—a fool despises almost all good instruction. A sage once noted the reason we have one mouth and two ears is because our Lord intended us to listen twice as much as we speak. But a cartooned caricature would picture the fool with two mouths and one ear—with a hearing aid, turned off.

Foolish students penalize themselves for life by refusing to learn while they have opportunity to do so.

When asked where he went to school Dr. Kenneth McFarland doesn't talk of his Ph.D.from Columbia. Instead he says, "I went to Miss Sadie Brown in the fifth grade at Camey, Kansas. One day she said, 'Kenneth, you're growing tall, but are you thinking tall? Son, there's a ladder resting on the floor of this schoolroom that goes as high as you want to go, but it starts right here!' Then she said, 'Don't you ever look upon this school as something you want to get out of. You get down on your knees every day and thank God you have this school to get into'."

Only a fool despises instruction. Wise are the teachable.

The foolish man who places too much stock in himself usually worships things.

Luke 12 quotes Jesus' story of a man whose ambition for wealth had been reached. "I have arrived," he announced. "This is what I have dreamed, schemed and sweated for. Now I can live it up. I've got it made." At that moment God tapped him on the shoulder and said, "Thou fool, this night thy soul is required of thee. Then what will happen to your things?" many a man who labels himself successful is judged a failure on eternity's scales because he let life's furniture make a fool of him.

Have you heard this?

"A man must live! We justify
Low shift and trick to treason high:
A little vote for a little gold,
Or a whole city bought and sold.
With this self evident reply,
A man must live!
But is it so? Pray tell me why
Life at such cost you have to buy.
In what religion were you told
A man must live?
There are times when a man must die!
There are times when a man will die!
Imagine for a battle-cry
From soldiers with a sword to hold,
From soldiers with a flag unfurled,
This coward's whine. This liar's lie,
A man must live.
The Saviour did not live, He died!
But in His death was life.
Life for Himself and all mankind.
He found His life by losing it.
And, we being crucified afresh with Him
May find life in the cup of death,
And drinking it, win life forever more!"

—*Charlotte Perkins Gilman*

III. One other characteristic of a fool by God's standard must be noted. He looks down on others. He lacks respect for his fellowmen.

Jesus said, "But I say unto you, that whosoever is angry with his brother without a cause shall be in danger of the judgment. And whosoever shall say to his brother 'Raca' shall be in danger of hell fire." (Matt. 5:22)

The word translated means "moral fool." It means you are accusing him of moral wrong-doing. You are slandering his character, you are ruining his reputation. To do this is to put yourself in danger of hell fire.

Other words for the gossip who would slander the character of another are found in Proverbs 10:18: "He that hideth hatred with lying lips and he that uttereth slander is a fool."

All who make trouble, who cause contention, are faced with Proverbs 18:6: "A fool's lips enter into contention and his mouth calleth for strokes." " His mouth calleth for strokes." Isn't that a great line? A troublemaker's mouth begs for a beating. One translation says: "His words endanger him."

From all this, one thing is certain. We are not to be trouble making gossips. Only a fool looks down on another creature made in God's image.

The Apostle Paul tells us that Christians are called "fools" by the world. Just as immoral people are among the first to accuse others of immorality, even so, the foolish are so very prone to call others foolish. Accepting that, Paul told the Christians at Corinth: "I am more than willing to be a fool for Christ's sake." (II Cor. 4:10)

Along Fifth Avenue in New York City walked a man wearing one of those walking billboard contraptions — you know, with a sign on the front and one on the back. As he approached people on the street some would laugh, others were offended, and still others felt pity, for on the front sign was lettered, "I am a fool for Christ's sake." But their moods changed as he passed by, for on the back panel they read: "Whose fool are you?"

CHAPTER FOUR

The Bible and Your Motivation

Have you noticed that every time something is done, someone did it? Have you ever asked: "Why not me?"

Exodus 32:1-5

Have you noticed that every time something is done, someone did it? And have you ever had a glimpse of glory that whispers, "Other people are doing great things, making things happen, why not me?" Well, why not?

In every organization, especially in the church of our Lord Jesus Christ, there are three kinds of people — those who make things happen, those who watch things happen and those who don't even know anything is happening.

Canada and Switzerland combined couldn't hold all the spiritual draft dodgers whose names are on the church rolls but have lost their way down life's tiresome and dusty detours. They are tired, bored, scared and lonely. They frantically seek happiness in bottles, needles, pills, thrills and games. They have found that the world's pick-me-ups always let them down. Some of these people come to church sit through nervously clocked hours of religious entertainment, often finding it not very entertaining and plod out the back door, thinking, "I didn't get anything out of that." Inscribe this indelibly on your heart, as long as you approach everything from the standpoint of what you are going to get out of it, then, my friend, you will miss life. You will never make things happen, you won't even have the ability to see things happen, you will walk right by a million miracles and not even know anything is happening.

Also in the church, are those who watch things happen. Content to be spectators, they are happy to see the victories and crushed by the defeats. They are definitely on the Lord's side. They sit in the stands, wave their pennants and give three cheers for Jesus.

All the while our Lord is calling us to the field, pleading with us to put on the equipment and get in the game.

And there are the folk of faith who make things happen. Shiloh Terrace is full of people like this.

Sunday School teachers who really love the people they teach. One of our men was driving past the home of a young man in his Sunday School class. This good teacher felt constrained to stop and visit one more time with the lost lad. That visit resulted in a soul being saved.

Outreach Leaders who know that if people are going to be reached, they are responsible for leading the way.

This church has a Day Care program and Kindergarten because this is a church of caring people—who make things happen.

We have people who give away time and love to children at Buckner's Orphans Home. One of our men is collecting and repairing old radios so each child can have his own radio in his room.

I know and admire one of our hard working men who goes every Thursday evening to lead a group of boys in a detention home in Bible study.

Every time someone has called, saying something like: "Preacher, we need help. I know it's a lot to ask, but could you send someone to sit up tonight with my sick husband?" I have called men who gave up their sleep to minister in the name of Christ.

And what about our young people? They share our great Good News everywhere. Recently many of them spent a holiday witnessing at Love Field and downtown. Our young people have been instrumental in starting chapels in every area high school and most junior high schools. Almost a hundred of them worked to earn the money so they could go to Minnesota and work and witness to people they didn't even know. Several adults gave up their vacations and made that trip on school buses and slept, what little they did sleep, on cots.

Know what? I haven't even scratched the surface. There are Christian people in this church doing things for Christ most of us don't even know about.

The joy of watching and working with people who, because they really care, make things happen is one of this pastor's highest pleasures.

How do you get to be the kind of person God uses? How do you come out of the stands and get in the game? How do you stop being a "Go get 'em team, three cheers for Jesus Christian" and become a "we'll work 'till Jesus comes" kind of Christian? These things must take place: become awake to God's leadership. Be aware that God will work through you. Be available so He can do exciting things with your life.

The third chapter of Exodus begins an account of how God calls and uses just one man. It tells how He communicates His way and provides His strength to those who want to be a part of what He is doing.

I. It All Begins When We Become Awake to God's Leadership.

Moses was on the backside of the desert and saw a bush burning. He soon became aware that through this burning bush God was saying something to him. Others would look and say, "Wow, look, a bush is burning." Moses looked and saw God. What makes the difference? Does this not say that you and I need to be developing a Christian sixth sense of awareness of God?

One poet said, "Earth is crowned with heaven and every bush aflame with God. But only those who see, take off their shoes. The rest sit around and pluck blackberries."

"Only those who see." Let us all pray for the wisdom to see.

Remember how the Israelites had a "God in a box" complex? They carried that Ark of the Covenant around and thought that God was nowhere but in that box. People still get caught in that kind of fuzzy thinking today, only they think we have made the box bigger and installed pews.

Yet the people He did things through were folks like Moses, who could see Him on the backside of a desert in a burning bush.

Or Job, who could sit suffering on a pile of ashes and have an experience with God.

Or Jonah, who knew he could repent in the belly of a whale.

Or Paul and Silas, who sang praises and prayed in a Philippian jail at midnight because they knew God was there.

Or John, banished from a church house forever, in a slave mining camp on the Isle of Patmos, and there received the vision from God that is inscribed in the Book of Revelation.

On two occasions God has been so real to me it radically altered my Christian life. One was in a beautiful church service. The pastor's sermon was entitled, "My Friend Jesus," and Jesus became a better friend to me than ever before. The other time was on a Sunday morning too, I think. I was not in church, but rather in a hot, dirty ditch, changing targets on a rifle range at Ft. Knox, Kentucky.

Learn to be aware that you may confront God in an unusual way—anywhere.

Songs we sing in church can become His very personal messages.

You know, I actually get letters saying my sermons have changed lives. That is fantastically amazing to me, until I realize that God can use anything to say something to people, sometimes even my sermons. You see, there wasn't anything unusual about that bush in the desert. It wasn't a special bush. In fact any old bush would do. I dare say that you may have been God's special messenger to someone in days gone by, or maybe even today.

Pray to be awake to God's leadership.

II. Secondly, Be Aware That God Will Work Through You.

Moses, like you and me, had some problems here. He just couldn't see how a sheepherder could be qualified for the position our Lord was offering him.

He made excuses—O how he made excuses! He said everything most nominating committees for Sunday School workers have heard.

In verse eleven: "Who am I that I should do this?"

"You're somebody who is going to have me with you," said God.

"What shall I say?" (Verse 13).

"Tell them I sent you."

"I'm not eloquent, I can't speak well." (4:10).

"Who made your mouth, Moses?"

"Lord, you've got to get somebody else." (4:13)

Then God was angry. That's how you make God angry.

After all this was over, Moses discovered a great thing. God *was* with him. God *did* speak through him and God was *all he needed* to become one of the best known men of all ages.

He wants to do so many great things through you. He wants so much for you.

You football fans, have you noticed how the best coaches love those players, pull for them and are so excited when one excels?

In a much higher way, God feels like this toward us. He has placed so much potential in each of us.

You have read how we use so little of our mental ability. In every way He has endowed us with abilities that our unbelief and negative attitudes keep us from developing. How He must be pained by an "I can't do it" negative attitude.

For instance, you recall that a few years ago everybody knew a human couldn't run a mile in less than four minutes. They knew it was impossible to run that fast, that long. That is, everybody knew it but Roger Bannister and he went out and ran a mile in three minutes and fifty-nine seconds. Now, since they know it can be done, men run a mile in less than four minutes all the time.

The song "High Hopes" has a line: "Everybody knows an ant can't move a rubber tree plant." But the ant believes he can and the next line states, "Oops, there goes another rubber tree plant!"

Never forget, God has put in us the ability to do anything He wants done.

Paul knew it, he testified in Philippians 4:13., "I can do all things through Christ who strengtheneth me."

III. The Secret to Uncovering All This Great Strength Is Availability. Just Make Yourself Available so God Can Work Through You.

Moses realized God was talking to him through the bush and he said, "Here am I."

Are you anxious to see God do something? Then let Him do it through you.

Have you heard this?

Jesus hid in a book
Isn't worth a second look.
Jesus buried in a creed
Is a helpless Christ, indeed.
But Jesus in the hearts of men
Shows His saving power again.

All you have to do is say, "Lord, here am I. I know you want to use me. I know you can use me and now I want you to know that I want you to use me."

CHAPTER FIVE

The Bible and Your Attitude

Here is a first-person account of how the greatest man who ever lived dramatically demonstrated true greatness to His success-hungry followers.

John 13:1-7 — I Peter 5:5, 6

It is June in Sinope, that city located on a peninsula on the south shore of the Black Sea, as though it were trying to peek across the waters at the unknown lands to the north. It is a good time of the year, climate-wise, in this place that is cold most of the time. But in June the temperature stays around 70 degrees, kept steady by the massive influence of the Black Sea.

The group at church had been looking forward to this meeting for some time. Months ago the news had reached them that Silas, the much-traveled companion of Paul and Peter, was coming to bring a letter of encouragement and instruction from the Apostle Peter. Silas had greeted Andrew, the brother of Simon Peter, who had been at Sinope for a while leading the people to a better knowledge of Christ. Silas read in clear tones the message addressed to the Christians of Pontus, Galatia, Cappadocia, Asia and Bithynia. After the meeting there was that warm Christian fellowship that means more than can be measured. Presently Silas excused himself and retired to a room prepared for him. It had been a long journey. Starting at Pontus, that far-out province on the southeast shore of the Black Sea, down through Galatia, south and west to the other Christian centers and now back north, across the arid country of Bithynia. It was refreshing to get back to the coast, especially in June, But he was tired.

Downstairs the people were still buzzing. Andrew was particularly happy to hear this word from his brother and to know that, at least for the time, Peter was still safe and sound and alive, and to hear another expression of his growing dedication to the Master.

One of the men snapped his chain of thought with the question, "Brother Andrew, we have been discussing the letter Silas read to us tonight. What do you think Peter had in mind when he said, '. . . Be clothed with humility . . . for God resisteth the proud and giveth grace to the humble'?"

"Ah, yes," said Andrew, "I am sure where he got that! All of us who walked with the Master those three years learned that lesson simultaneously and strikingly. Sit down, man, and I'll tell you about it.

"We were back in Jerusalem for the last time. Those delightful, yet difficult and distressing months of walking the dusty roads with Him were drawing to an end. We had been sharers, but mostly spectators of this matchless miracle worker's ministry. Things were coming to a head. The Pharisees, especially, were determined to be rid of Him. Amidst all the clamor and threats on His life, He led us back to Jerusalem, the most dangerous place for Him to be and also for us. We were all sure that the time was come. Surely this will be the climax, we thought, in which He will declare His kingdom and overthrow the cruel Caesar whose arrogant legionnaires had spilled into every Jewish city.

"You see, we misunderstood Christ, even though, under any circumstances we were willing to follow Him. In spite of walking with Him and trying to catch step with Him and seeking to be good followers of His, for those three years plus, we still missed by a long sea mile, His purpose in coming. We were expecting a physical rule, a military Messiah who would throw off this Roman yoke of bondage. We were looking for temporal freedom and He had come to give us eternal liberty. We wanted to be free from Rome and He came to make us free from ourselves, our sins. We wanted to walk the streets of Jerusalem as free men and He gave us the privilege of knowing that we can walk the streets of heaven as forgiven men. We had yet to learn that anyone under the bondage of sin is the real slave. That even so great a power as Rome will one day lie in ruins because anything or anyone dominated by sin is temporary, corruptible!

"I have often reflected upon this missing the mark in understanding Him. Looking back it is so easy to see that He was telling us about a Spiritual Kingdom all along. I'll never be able to thank Him enough for that cross, that supreme sacrifice for my sins, but when I think of how He put up with us, with me, those years, I am amazed. I don't know what to admire the most, His passion for me or His patience with me—His suffering on the cross or His longsuffering with my dull understanding.

"But we hadn't perceived this Spiritual Kingdom yet, and expecting to be rewarded in this 'kingdom' we anticipated for three years service we had rendered, each one began to think about the high places of leadership we would surely assume.

"In fact, there was dissension in the ranks over who was going to be big dog—hold the high position. It all came out in the open when the Mother of James and John came to Christ and plainly asked that her sons be given the number one and two spots. Of course, we had been thinking about this all along. I guess there's a sort of Caesar complex in every heart.

"On this particular night Christ had prepared for us to have one of those very rare moments alone with Him. He had secured from a friend the use of an upper room so that we might observe the Passover feast. We were certain that tonight He would assign the positions.

"It is customary, as you know, for the wealthy to have a servant at the door to remove your sandals and to wash the dust off your feet. Of course, we were not a wealthy bunch and with the very few exceptions when we dined with someone like Zacchaeus, we did this service for each other. But on this night none was willing to play the role of a servant. No one wanted to appear subordinate to the others in the eyes of Christ. We had walked much that day and our feet were especially dirty, but we removed our sandals and took our places at the table.

"At this point I noticed something was different about Christ. I can't explain it, but somehow His eyes were more piercing, His bearing more commanding, His very countenance radiated authority. Now I realized that Christ knew that all power in heaven and on earth had been put into His hands, that He had received the very Power of God.

"Have you ever dreamed about what you would do, if suddenly you became powerful because of money or reputation or position? Of course, you have. The desire to be drum major invades even the bass drum bearer at times. But here was the real thing! He had all power, all authority—what would He do with it? He knew full well what was ahead, that He soon would be leaving us. Why not stage something vividly dramatic to imprint indelibly upon us who He was? Why not take a robe, place a crown on His head and call upon us to kneel down before the Lord of all to whom the Father had given all authority? Not a scepter He takes, but a towel, pours water into a basin, washes our grimy feet one by one and dries them with the towel.

"Now Christ was always doing the unusual, especially when the usual was useless or wrong. He drove an ox cart through all of the worn traditions of the dead faith of our day. And He cast out demons with no regard for other people's pigs.

"Yes, we had sort of grown to expect the unexpected, but this night, bless you, we were all caught off guard! Here the Lord, the Master, the One we knew to be the Christ, was doing for us a menial task we would not do for each other.

"He had wrapped that towel around His waist—no one did that but slaves—and Him. As he began to wash our feet we were so quiet you could hear the leaves rustle in the gentle breeze outside the window. First He washed the feet of Judas, even though He knew Judas was going to betray Him. A year before He told us that one of us would do it. Had he known all along? Next the feet of John and James, still not a word. But when He knelt before my brother, Simon broke the silence with that booming voice of his, that matches his hulk.

" 'Lord, are you going to wash my feet?'

"And Jesus answered, 'You don't understand what I'm doing now, but soon you will.'

" 'You'll never wash my feet like a slave,' said Peter.

"Tenderly Jesus stated, 'If I don't wash you, you have no part with me.'

" 'Then wash not only my feet but my face and hands,' said a submissive Simon Peter.

" 'No, he that already has been washed, needs only that his feet be washed,' and looking around he asserted, 'And you are washed, but not all of you.' He said this because Judas was still there.

"Do you catch the spiritual meaning here? As Jesus had said, His own are already clean because they are His. This act was symbolic of whatever is necessary to clean up defilement contracted on the way. We have seen the Romans go to their public baths, then walk back to their houses. The last thing they do before going inside to take off the robe and dress is to wash off the dust they have gotten on their feet during the walk from the bath house to their home. Christ said, 'You are clean because I have cleansed you. But you still have to walk in a dirty world and you will be picking up that dirt and you ought to let me wash it off.'

"He finished the task, washing and drying our feet. Putting on His outer garment, He asked a question, not near so simple as it sounded, 'Do you know what I have done?' Already He had told Peter he didn't know.

" 'You have called me Master and Lord and that is right, for so I am. If your Lord and Master has washed your feet you ought also to wash each other's feet.'

"We knew He wasn't starting a new ordinance. We knew He had shown us that our yearning for greatness, by our standards, was wrong. He had stripped Himself of dignity, taken the lowliest place of a slave, to serve us, in our highest interests—so we ought to strip ourselves of all our dignities, and take the lowliest place of service, in His highest interest.

"Why hadn't we really heard before? He had said it—'He that is greatest of all shall be servant of all.' This is God's idea of greatness. He has become involved in humanity and in the historical process then there is no future for the tyrant or for the boss because when God came He took the form of a servant. The only future is with Him who is willing to take the form of a servant. Now we know what He meant when He said, "The meek shall inherit the earth." The meek, not the great or the powerful or the cultured but the meek!"

This is the truth. If you would be a follower of Christ, then you must be His servant. You may believe anything about Him you like, and it may be orthodox, and you may be in good standing with your church and you may have the heart of a pagan. Because what saves us is not our idea of Christ, but whether we have given ourselves in commitment to that crucified and living Lord.

"Forgive me, I know I've kept you longer than you bargained for, but a willing ear is a preacher's greatest encouragement. That is the story behind the statement of my Brother. This was the scene that prompted him to charge us to 'clothe ourselves with humility.' We saw our Lord do it that night and we heard Him tell us and all who will follow Him to do the same."

Did you notice the word for "clothe" Simon used? The same word applies to the garment of a slave and also the garment of a prince. We saw the garment of slavery on Jesus, and before He was through it seemed it was the garment of royalty. Now this word is written to young, old, all of us. "Put on humility as a slave's garment, and so learn to wear the garment of true royalty."

We learned this when the greatest One of all showed us how it is done, that to be servant is really to be sovereign.

CHAPTER SIX

The Bible and Your Assurance

Success in an up-tight age must include the ability to be calm and confident.

I John 1:5-7

Up-tight is a very popular description of people's feelings these days. It means the same thing as "tense" or "on edge." Up-tight people are under stress. They lose their "cool" or calmness quite easily. They are not able to "hang loose" and enjoy life. One wit said: "America used to be called a melting pot, but now it has become a pressure cooker."

What causes the pressure? Whence comes the up-tightness? There are several causes—feelings of guilt, not being certain about where life is headed, and lack of a solid foundation to build life upon.

Up-tight folks are practical atheists. Oh, they probably would be offended at being called practical atheists, many even go to church. Yet the fact is, they have no real god but themselves. Their creed could be stated: "I think I can, all by myself." Their philosophy is aptly put in a poem that has become immortal because it reflects the belief of so many in this up-tight age. The poem "Invictus":

Out of the night that covers me,
Black as a pit from pole to pole,
I thank whatever gods may be
For my unconquerable soul.

In the fell clutch of circumstance
I have not winced nor cried aloud.
Under the bludgeonings of chance
My head is bloody but unbowed.

Beyond this place of wrath and tears
Looms but the horror of the shade.
Yet the menace of the years
Finds and shall find me unafraid.

It matters not how strait the gate,
How charged with punishment the scrolls.
I am the Master of my fate,
I am the Captain of my soul.

Do you see how much pressure a position like that places on a person? To say, "I am the Master of my fate, I am the Captain of my soul" is to say, "I am my God!" Live with that for a while and you become extremely up-tight because there will always be a gnawing awareness that you are not big enough to be your god. That's just not enough foundation to build anything substantial upon. Some of those foundations are getting big cracks in them. Even the author of "Invictus" had to face up to it; he was not big enough to be his master nor wise enough to be his captain and in utter despair, he took his own life.

Jesus came to tell up-tight people that they can be free—free to live—free to enjoy—free to have life abundant.

He tells us there is an answer to being up-tight. You can be upright. That means you can be in good standing with God again. Your sins can be forgiven and forgotten. You can know that some day when you stand before God your name is on a list guaranteeing your reservation in heaven. You can have Christ living in you here to help you face every temptation, handle every difficulty and guide in every decision. When you are upright, in good standing with God, you do not have to be up-tight.

Being right with God is so important that the book of I John is in the Bible as a sort of check-list, so people can examine their faith. In Chapter 1, verses five through seven, God spells out what uprightness really involves. It is made pointedly plain that right standing with Him means commitment to God; it involves a community, a fellowship with other Christians; and it comes only through a cleansing of sin by Jesus Christ.

I. Right Standing With God Involves a Commitment to God.

He is completely good. "God is light, and in Him is no darkness at all." We can have every confidence in Him. He never does anything from hidden motives.

Everything He does is because He is Love and He is Good and He is Truth. He does not trick you. He really wants you to have the best kind of life that never ends.

It is important to know God is good because it is His will that we give all of our life to Him. "If we say we have fellowship with Him and walk in darkness, we lie and do not know the truth." You see, the Bible says there is a big connection between believing and behaving. If we believe in a good God then we will want to be good people.

Verse six plainly states that those who really know God will walk, that is, will live their every step in a manner pleasing to God. The Bible also is saying that those who say they know God, but do not live godly lives are living a lie. This does not mean that you are deliberately lying. It may be you have been deceived, you have believed a lie. There are two very common and very false ideas about our faith that must be corrected.

The first thing you must not believe is that you can isolate God. You must not think of worshiping God as going to a certain place to do certain things. Real worship is a life committed to Him—daily walked according to His will.

For all too many worship is going to a certain building on Sunday morning. You wear nice clothes. You say nice things. Very few would be crude enough to curse or tell smutty jokes or gossip about others in the church building because it is God's house, the place where God is. The barber shop is different. The beauty parlor is different. There is no conviction that God is there. The office, the plant, the store, the school is different. No one thinks much of God being there.

If that is the way you approach life, my friend, then you are believing a lie. The truth is, God is everywhere. A Christian has a great need for fellowship and worship and he is also aware that God is with him each moment of each day. The highest act of worship is in living those days for Him.

Have you noticed that the stories Jesus told never dealt with how to act in church? Rather they told how, because of our faith, we are to act outside of church.

There is another thing you must not believe. You must not think that becoming a Christian is only accepting as truth some facts about Jesus Christ. Would you agree with me that the Devil is not a Christian? Yet the Devil believes that Christ is the son of God. He believes that Jesus died on the cross for the sins of mankind. He believes that Christ rose from the dead. In fact, he not only believes these things about Christ, he knows them to be true, he saw it happen. Yet the Devil is not a Christian. Just knowing facts about Jesus is not enough.

The Bible tells us what Jesus said to people who wanted to receive His eternal life. They did have to get the facts straight, but after they did, then He said: "Follow me." In Matthew 16 He asked, "Who are people saying that I am?" We must know who He is, but that is not enough. In verse 24 He goes on to say: "If any man will come after me let him deny himself, take up his cross and follow me." In John 21 He said three times to Simon: "Do you love me?" Three times Simon Peter said he did love Jesus, but that was not enough. In verse 19 Jesus said, "Then follow me."

We must always keep in mind that Christianity is not primarily an institution, an organization, an ideal, a way of life, an impersonal movement. These are all secondary. Christianity is, most of all, an allegiance to a person and that person is Jesus Christ. He asks: "What do you think of me?" and "Do you love me?" and always He says, "Follow me."

Remember the book, *In His Steps?* It is a story of ordinary people who become extraordinary because they faced every opportunity, every decision, every day with the question, "What would Jesus do?" That is how we are to follow Him.

II. Right standing with God not only involves commitment, it also includes community with other Christians. "But if we walk in the light as He is in the light, we have fellowship one with another."

The Word of God is here asserting that Christian people will seek fellowship with other Christians.

You have heard it said: "Birds of a feather flock together." A statement like that puts all too much emphasis on what color the feathers are. It is true, however, that people of a common commitment commune together. If we really love Him and want to please Him and serve Him then we will want to be with other people who feel the same way.

The word "fellowship" means partnership—people who share in the same kind of life, the same kind of goals.

A church is a place where those who love God come because they also love each other. In the church we do not pretend to be something we are not. We do not pass judgment on other people. We care about each other and all others. Historians of the first century noted with amazement that those beginning believers really did love each other.

III. For one who is upright there is a commitment, a community and a cleansing. "And the blood of Jesus Christ, His Son, cleanseth us from all sin."

The words we have looked at in this passage are addressed to Christians. They remind us that even as Christians, we stumble and fall, but the blood, the life that Christ laid down for us, keeps on cleansing us from our sins, keeps on washing the dirt out of our systems.

But what if you're not a Christian? You say, "I don't think I can live a committed life. And quite honestly, I don't much like church." There is nothing sinful or evil about either of those statements. You are just being honest with God. The truth is, you cannot live a committed life without Christ's help. There is no reason why you should enjoy church if you are not a Christian. The Bible agrees: "The preaching of the word is foolishness to them that perish."

This is the great thing about becoming a Christian. You don't have to pretend. You don't have to put on an act. You can come to God honestly just as you are.

People are up-tight because they have tried to fool themselves. They have been trying to say wrong is right and dark is light and it just has not worked. A man from another city told me last week of two young women who tried to tell themselves that the pleasure-seeking "new morality" is the way to live and their guilt feelings caused so much up-tighteness they each attempted suicide.

When you come to Christ you can honestly lay it all on the line and He will accept you and change you. Christianity is revolutionary. It changes people. The change is so revolutionary it is like starting all over again.

Carl Jung, the famous psychiatrist, spoke of Christianity as adding a new rung on the ladder of evolution. It "has produced on earth a new creature who lives in a new way to which the natural man can no more attain than a crawling thing can learn to fly."

That is exactly what the Bible asserts. John said, "And as many as received Him to them gave He power to become sons of God." Paul stated, "If any man be in Christ, he is a new creature. Old things are passed away, behold all things are become new."

Here is the good news of Christianity. If you want life, stop trying to achieve it. Let God give it to you. Come to Him through Jesus Christ and He will cleanse you of your sins. He will make you a new creature so you can live a life of commitment to Him. He will make you one of His family, people who love each other, need each other and care about each other.

Most of all, when you come to Him, He takes the pressure off. Because of Him you are no longer up-tight, now you are upright. I shared "Invictus" with you at the beginning of this message. Let me close with a Christian's answer to "Invictus":

Out of the light that dazzles me,
Bright as the sun from pole to pole,

I thank the God I know to be
For Christ, the Conqueror of my soul.

Since He's the sway of circumstance
I would not wince nor cry aloud.
Under that rule which men call "chance"
My head with joy is humbly bowed.

Beyond this place of sin and tears,
That life with Him, and He's the aid,
That, spite the menace of the years
Keeps and shall keep me unafraid.

It matters not, though strait the gate,
He cleared from punishment the scroll.
Christ is the Master of my fate,
Christ, the Captain of my soul!

—*Author Unknown*

CHAPTER SEVEN

The Bible and Your Commitment

No team ever scored by staying in the huddle.

Several years ago, Andy Griffith created no small stir in the entertainment world with a record entitled, "What It Was Was Football." He portrayed a "country boy come to town" who saw his first game of football. The field was seen as a "pretty little cow pasture" on which someone had planted posts and painted stripes. The game itself he described as "two bunches of men fighting over a little pumpkin." His conclusion was that the object of the game is to move that little pumpkin from one end of that cow pasture to the other without getting knocked down or stepping in something."

You and I have watched football, too and we are aware that the huddle is not the most exciting part. Yet the huddle is very important to the team. This is when the assignments are made. Through days of practice and study each player knows what he is supposed to do to execute a play. In the huddle, the quarterback, who has been designated by the coach to be the leader on the field, encourages the players to do their best, calls the play and then they all go to the line of scrimmage to face the opposition.

One day Jesus took Peter, James and John to the top of the mountain for a very special huddle. The Bible says that He was transformed or changed. The word literally means that His outward appearance reflected His inner nature. During that time what He was really like on the inside, showed on the outside. Of course, this made a deep and lasting impression on the Apostles with Him. John said, in the first words of his gospel, "We beheld His glory, the glory of the only begotten of the Father, full of grace and truth." Since He was full of God's grace and truth on the inside that glory shone from His face and even reflected from His clothing. In these days, when airlines advertise, "If you've got it, flaunt it," yet the policy of so many is, "If you haven't got it, fake it." It is sort of frightening to think that what is on the inside would show up on the outside. The Bible states that His clothing became more dazzlingly white than any earthly process could make it. Scientists are always admitting that God does a better job. Our sonar is not as good as the dolphin's. Bats have much better radar equipment built into their tiny bodies than we can put into giant buildings. Now the Scripture is saying that He can make clothes brilliantly white without enzymes, chlorine or borax!

To add to the frightening wondrousness of this great moment, there appeared Moses and Elijah and they talked at length with Christ. Don't you know our Lord was so very hungry for fellowship with folks like that? And how much He had missed it since coming to earth?

This time of talking between Moses, Elijah and Jesus was interrupted by Simon Peter. Simon was so frightened that his mind was disengaged, his wits were frozen, but his mouth worked wondrously. He said, "Lord, this is what we're going to do. This is a beautiful place, we're having a great time here, let's build three shelters, one for you, one for Moses and one for Elijah." Have you noticed that when a preacher doesn't know what else to do he wants to build something?

Suddenly there was a cloud hanging overhead. This was a different kind of cloud. Instead of casting a shadow, it created light. From that cloud the voice of God interrupted Peter's interruption to say, "This is my dearly beloved Son, listen to Him."

Just that quickly it was over. Peter, James and John were lying prone on the ground, faces down, scared to death, afraid to look. Jesus bent down and touched them and said, "Don't be afraid, get up, it is time to go."

When they got to the valley they found a scene of defeat and despair. A distraught father had brought his very seriously ill son to be healed by the other nine Apostles. They had been unable to do it and gleefully the Pharisees had seized upon this opportunity to discredit Christ and His message. Isn't that sad? Those supposedly religious people were delighted that the boy could not be healed. I heard a story I sure hope is not true of a preacher who had returned from a revival in a two-church community. When someone asked, "Did you have a good meeting?" He replied, "No, but thank goodness the Methodists didn't either.' That's the Pharisee spirit.

Then the people looked up and saw Christ. Isn't it fantastic to know that in the difficult times we can look up and see Christ? He always comes down to the valley where there is need. What mixed emotions they had. They were ashamed for their failure yet delighted to see Him.

Notice that Jesus asked what the problem was and immediately began dealing with the father of the sick boy. He is never interested in debating with the critics, He wants to deal with the one who has a problem.

Of course, the boy was healed and the Disciples learned a great lesson in spiritual depth and preparation.

From this exciting story of contrasts between the mountain of inspiration and the valley of defeat we learn when it's time to leave the huddle.

I. It is important that we get in the huddle. You're not even in the game if you're not in the huddle.

The huddle is a time of information and inspiration and planning of strategy. We need these meetings of Christians together, away from the world.

That's why Jesus took those three men with Him upon that mountain. It was a time of information, inspiration and a further development of His strategy to make a way back to God for a lost world.

It is interesting to note what Moses and Elijah and our Lord talked about. Do you ever listen to yourself and other people talk? Do it sometime. Very interesting. As we listen to what people talk about and combine that with what we know about heaven, I wonder if most people will have anything at all to say. It is highly unlikely that we will spend our time running down the administration. We won't be able to shake our heads and talk about how heaven is going to the dogs and how it used to be in the good old days. The weather will be perfect. We will not talk about our aches and pains because we won't have any. We shall not gossip or snipe at others because the Lord is going to remove that poison from our system. Well, take away gunning at the establishment—griping about the mess things are in—growling about the weather—groaning about aches and pains and gossiping about others and you've just about eliminated the totality of some folk's conversational ability.

When we look at what these three men from heaven talked about it will give us an idea of how conversation will go in heaven and also tell us what we ought to talk about in our Christian huddles here on earth.

Luke 9:31 tells us that they spoke of Jesus' death on the cross. Have you noticed that is the thing most everyone in the Bible talked about. The cross and the resurrection is the theme of the Bible—Christ came to die for our sins and rose to prove His victory.

What should we talk about in Heaven? The cross and His love. What should we talk about when we come together here on earth? The cross and Him who died thereon.

Moses and Elijah talked about the cross.

John the Baptist said, "Behold the Lamb of God that taketh away the sins of the world." He was talking about the cross.

Isaiah prophesied, "He was wounded for our transgressions, He was bruised for our iniquities."

John said, "The blood of Jesus Christ, His Son cleanseth us from all sin."

Peter preached, "Ye were not redeemed with corruptible things, as silver and gold, but with the precious blood of Christ."

Paul proclaimed, "God forbid that I should glory save in the death of our Lord Jesus Christ."

In the Revelation vision John heard the cross as the theme of the angel's song: "Worthy is the Lamb that was slain." To talk of the cross is heavenly language.

The old song should be our testimony: "I Love to Tell the Story—Twill Be My Theme in Glory to Tell the Old, Old Story of Jesus and His Love." That's what we should talk about. That's what we will talk about.

II. When we are in the huddle we should be preparing ourselves for the work God wants us to do. We should learn the assignments.

Yet instead of getting the assignment from our Lord we are prone to spend our time telling the Lord what we want to do. Isn't that incredible? Instead of getting our instructions from Him we go our merry little way telling the Lord how we will serve Him.

Peter is our prototype in this strange activity. During that high and splendid time of fellowship between Moses, Elijah and Jesus, the Bible states that "Peter answered and said." But Peter was answering when he hadn't been asked. He was speaking when he had not been spoken to. And when he says, "Let us build three tabernacles . . . " he was not asking for permission, he was telling the Lord what they were going to do. He was saying, "This is what we are going to do, this is a wonderful place. This is better than Glorieta, Falls Creek and Paisano rolled into one. Let's stay on this mountain."

A while ago I said the old song, "I Love to Tell the Story," ought to hit at the heart of Christian conversation. Another "golden oldie" my mother said they always sang at the Sunday meeting at Spring Creek is entitled, "Beulah Land." The words: "Far away the noise of strife upon my ear is falling . . . I'm living on the mountain, underneath a cloudless sky,

I'm drinking at the fountain that never shall run dry; for I am dwelling in Beulah Land."

From Simon Peter to now, the temptation of Christians is to find some place where they can retreat from the world and stay there, far away from the noise of strife. And we say, "Look, Lord, this is what we are going to do. Let's build a building here and we'll stay in this building. We will study how to witness, but we'll never leave the building to witness. We will read about what other missionaries are doing, but we will never be missionaries ourselves because we'd have to leave the building. We will sit in our air-conditioned comfort and tell ourselves we are the only ones who care. But we will not go out into the world and tell the people who are hurting and sick and lost that we care. We are dwelling in Beulah land."

But notice what happened. While Peter was talking, God stopped him and said, "This is my beloved Son. Don't tell Him what you are going to do. Listen to Him, and do what He tells you."

Then, why don't we listen to Him? Those whose idea of winning the lost is to say, "In four months we will schedule a revival and in that way we can say we are concerned without having to leave the building." Hear Him assert, "You say four months and then cometh the harvest. I say look on the fields for they are white already to harvest. And I need your help to gather the harvest. Go out into the fields where the harvest is."

It is vitally important to listen to what Christ said after His resurrection and before He ascended to heaven. It was during that very strategic time that He was giving the church her assignment. He emphasized two things: praying and witnessing. He said, "Tarry in Jerusalem until you are filled with the Spirit." Then His very last words were, "Ye shall receive power after the Holy Ghost is come upon you and ye shall be witnesses unto me." This is the way we are to fulfill His command, "Go ye therefore and make disciples."

III. So when we have come to the huddle, gotten our instructions, our inspiration and the assurance of His power, then we are to run the play.

Ignoring Peter's suggestion about the tabernacles and staying on the mountain, Jesus said, "Get up, it is time to go." And He led them down into the valley where people were needing Him.

An almost equal parallel in the life of our Lord preceded His death on the cross. He had taken these same three men into Gethsemane, a time of retreat and prayer. But after an hour He came, awoke His sleeping Disciples and said, "Get up, it is time to go," and He went out and died on the cross for us.

Our Lord wants us to come to the meetings. Hebrews 10:25 commands us not to forsake the assembling of ourselves together. But can't you hear Him saying, "Get up, it is time to go. It is time to do the thing I have called you to do. Go, tell the good news."

Do you remember that frigid day of the 1967 NFL Championship Game up in the cold, wilds of Wisconsin? The field was frozen and slick. The temperature was below zero, and the Dallas Cowboys had that championship snatched from their hands.

Do you recall that last drive, with the clock running out, how the Green Bay Packer fans, sitting in that biting cold urged their team in saying, "Go, Go, Go?"

The eleventh chapter of Hebrews tells of past heroes of the faith: Enoch, Noah, Abraham Moses and others. Then, Hebrews 12 begins: "Wherefore seeing we also are compassed about with so great a cloud of witnesses let us lay aside every weight and the sin that doth so easily beset us and let us run with patience the race that is set before us . . . "

The Bible is saying that you and I are on the field and the grandstand is filled with the faithful followers of God in years past. Peter, James, John, Moses, Elijah, Noah, Abraham and scores of others who have served Him are shouting to us saying, "Go, Go, Go!"

What a sin to stay in the huddle and lose the game by default.